Homeless In America

Table of Contents:

Why Are People Homeless? _____ page 2

Types of Homelessness _____ page 4

POVERTY _____ page 5
ERODING WORK OPPORTUNITIES _____ page 7
DECLINE IN PUBLIC ASSISTANCE _____ page 8

HOUSING _____ page 9

Criminalization of Homelessness _____ page 10

What can be done? _____ page 13

Resources _____ page 14

OTHER FACTORS _____ page 15

Homeless Bill of Rights _____ page 20

Why Are People Homeless?

As many as 3.5 million Americans are homeless each year. Of these, more than 1 million are children and on any given night, more than 300,000 children are homeless.

While the general impression is that the homeless are primarily the chronic and episodic, those unfortunate individuals often seen living on the streets in the downtown areas of our cities, the fact is that more than half the homeless are families with children. The vast majority of these have been thrust into homelessness by a life altering event or series of events that were unexpected and unplanned for. Contrary to the belief that homelessness is primarily the result of major traumatic events or physical and mental disabilities, there are many top causes of homelessness in America.

Homelessness is, in fact, caused by tragic life occurrences like the loss of loved ones, job loss, domestic violence, divorce and family disputes. Other impairments such as depression, untreated mental illness, post traumatic stress disorder, and physical disabilities are also responsible for a large portion of the homeless. Many factors push people into living on the street. Acknowledging these can help facilitate the end of homelessness in America.

For those living in poverty or close to the poverty line, an "everyday" life issue that may be manageable for individuals with a higher income can be the final factor in placing them on the street. A broken down vehicle, a lack of vehicle insurance, or even unpaid tickets might be just enough to render someone homeless.

Divorce costs and the associated lowering of a family's total income can cause one or more family members to become homeless. For families that can hardly pay their bills, a serious illness or disabling accident may deplete their funds and push them out onto the street. Today, the rapid, unexpected loss of jobs and resultant foreclosures has caused great dislocation among families and has dramatically added to the number of people without a roof over their heads.

Natural disasters often cause current housing situations to become untenable and costly repairs are often simply not possible. The results of Hurricane Katrina stand in bleak testimony to the power of nature to displace people.

The great challenge for the newly homeless is to figure out how to return to their normal lives. Organizations that build emergency shelters and transitional housing typically work with a larger number of service providers around the country whose mission is to provide the services, such as job training, social skills training, and financial training, that enable these people to regain employment and return to mainstream lives. The progression for these recently homeless is to first be housed in transitional residences where they can learn these skills, to graduate to assisted living in affordable housing while they build up economic reserves and rebuild their employment resume, and then to graduate to full, market rate housing.

Many of these service provider partners are household names, such as Volunteers of America, Rescue Missions, and the Salvation Army. Many others are local organizations formed to address specific homelessness issues in the community. By carefully vetting the qualifications and financial stability of these service providers, organizations that build emergency shelters and transitional housing are able to assure that their facilities are effectively utilized in the fight to end homelessness.

There are three types of homelessness – chronic, transitional, and episodic – which <u>can be defined</u> as follows:

Chronic Homelessness

- Persons most like the stereotyped profile of the "skid-row" homeless, who are likely to be entrenched in the shelter system and for whom shelters are more like long-term housing rather than an emergency arrangement. These individuals are likely to be older, and consist of the "hard-core unemployed", often suffering from disabilities and substance abuse problems. Yet such persons represent a far smaller proportion of the population compared to the transitionally homeless.

Transitional Homelessness

- Transitionally homeless individuals generally enter the shelter system for only one stay and for a short period. Such persons are likely to be younger, are probably recent members of the precariously housed population and have become homeless because of some catastrophic event, and have been forced to spend a short time in a homeless shelter before making a transition into more stable housing. Over time, transitionally homeless individuals will account for the majority of persons experiencing homelessness given their higher rate of turnover.

Episodic Homelessness

- Those who frequently shuttle in and out of homelessness are known as episodically homeless. They are most likely to be young, but unlike those in transitional homelessness, episodically homeless individuals often are chronically unemployed and experience medical, mental health, and substance abuse problems.

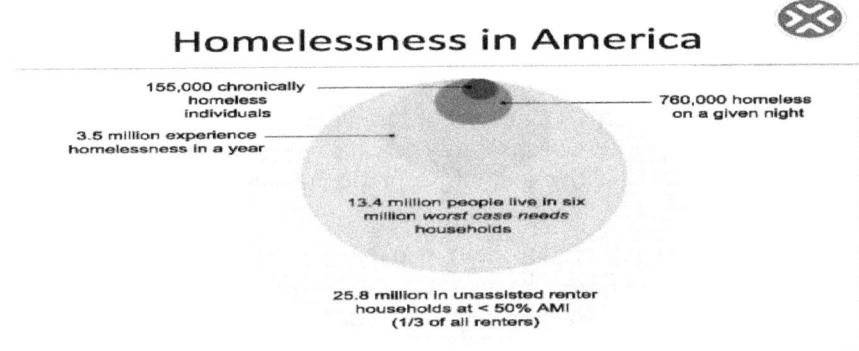

POVERTY

Homelessness and poverty are inextricably linked. Poor people are frequently unable to pay for housing, food, childcare, health care, and education. Difficult choices must be made when limited resources cover only some of these necessities. Often it is housing, which absorbs a high proportion of income that must be dropped. If you are poor, you are essentially an illness, an accident, or a paycheck away from living on the streets.

In 2011, the official poverty rate was 15.0%. There were 46.2 million people in poverty.

Two factors help account for increasing poverty:

Lack of Employment Opportunities – With unemployment rates remaining high, jobs are hard to find in the current economy. Even if people can find work, this does not automatically provide an escape from poverty.

Decline in Available Public Assistance – The declining value and availability of public assistance is another source of increasing poverty and homelessness and many families leaving welfare struggle to get medical care, food, and housing as a result of loss of benefits, low wages, and unstable employment. Additionally, most states have not replaced the old welfare system with an alternative that enables families and individuals to obtain above-poverty employment and to sustain themselves when work is not available or possible.

Other major factors, which can contribute to homelessness, include:

Lack of Affordable Health Care – For families and individuals struggling to pay the rent, a serious illness or disability can start a downward spiral into homelessness, beginning with a lost job, depletion of savings to pay for care, and eventual eviction.

- **Domestic Violence** – Battered women who live in poverty are often forced to choose between abusive relationships and homelessness. In addition, 50% of the cities surveyed by the U.S. Conference of Mayors identified domestic violence as a primary cause of homelessness (U.S. Conference of Mayors, 2005).
- **Mental Illness** – Approximately 16% of the single adult homeless population suffers from some form of severe and persistent mental illness (U.S. Conference of Mayors, 2005).
- **Addiction** – The relationship between addiction and homelessness is complex and controversial. Many people who are addicted to alcohol and drugs never become homeless, but people who are poor and addicted are clearly at increased risk of homelessness.

Homelessness and poverty are inextricably linked. Poor people are frequently unable to pay for housing, food, childcare, health care, and education. Difficult choices must be made when limited resources cover only some of these necessities. Often it is housing, which absorbs a high proportion of income that must be dropped. If you are poor, you are essentially an illness, an accident, or a paycheck away from living on the streets.

In 2007, 12.5% of the U.S. population, or 37,300,00 million people, lived in poverty. The official poverty rate in 2007 was not statistically different than 2006 (U.S. Bureau of the Census, 2007). Children are overrepresented, composing 35.7% of people in poverty while only being 24.8% of the total population.

Two factors help account for increasing poverty: eroding employment opportunities for large segments of the workforce and the declining value and availability of public assistance.

ERODING WORK OPPORTUNITIES

Reasons why homelessness persists include stagnant or falling incomes and less secure jobs which offer fewer benefits.

Low-wage workers have been particularly have been left behind as the disparity between rich and poor has mushroomed. To compound the problem, the real value of the minimum wage in 2004 was 26% less than in 1979 (The Economic Policy Institute, 2005). Factors contributing to wage declines include a steep drop in the number and bargaining power of unionized workers; erosion in the value of the minimum wage; a decline in manufacturing jobs and the corresponding expansion of lower-paying service-sector employment; globalization; and increased nonstandard work, such as temporary and part-time employment (Mishel, Bernstein, and Schmitt, 1999). To combat this, Congress has planned a gradual minimum wage increase, resulting in minimum wage raised to $9.50 by 2011.

Declining wages, in turn, have put housing out of reach for many workers: in every state, more than the minimum wage is required to afford a one- or two-bedroom apartment at Fair Market Rent. [1] A recent U.S. Conference of Mayors report stated that in every state more than the minimum-wage is required to afford a one or two-bedroom apartment at 30% of his or her income, which is the federal definition of affordable housing. Unfortunately, for 12 million Americans, more then 50% of their salaries go towards renting or housing costs, resulting in sacrifices in other essential areas like health care and savings.

The connection between impoverished workers and homelessness can be seen in homeless shelters, many of which house significant numbers of full-time wage earners. In 2007, a survey performed by the U.S. Conference of Mayors found that 17.4% of homeless adults in families were employed while 13% of homeless single adults or unaccompanied youth were employed. In the 2008 report, eleven out of nineteen cities reported an increased in employed homeless people.

With unemployment rates remaining high, jobs are hard to find in the current economy. Even if people can find work, this does not automatically provide an escape from poverty.

DECLINE IN PUBLIC ASSISTANCE

The declining value and availability of public assistance is another source of increasing poverty and homelessness. Until its repeal in August 1996, the largest cash assistance program for poor families with children was the Aid to Families with Dependent Children (AFDC) program. The Personal Responsibility and Work Opportunity Reconciliation Act of 1996 (the federal welfare reform law) repealed the AFDC program and replaced it with a block grant program called Temporary Assistance to Needy Families (TANF). In 2005, TANF helped a third of the children that AFDC helped reach above the 50% poverty line. Unfortunately, TANF has not been able to kept up with inflation. In 2006-2008, TANF case load has continued to decline while food stamp caseloads have increased.

Moreover, extreme poverty is growing more common for children, especially those in female-headed and working families. This increase can be traced directly to the declining number of children lifted above one-half of the poverty line by government cash assistance for the poor (Children's Defense Fund and the National Coalition for the Homeless, 1998).

As a result of loss of benefits, low wages, and unstable employment, many families leaving welfare struggle to get medical care, food, and housing.

People with disabilities, too, must struggle to obtain and maintain stable housing. In 2006, on a national average, monthly rent for a one-bedroom apartment rose to $715 per month which is a 113.1% of a person's on Supplemental Security Income (SSI) monthly income (Priced Out in 2006). For the first time, the national average rent for a studio apartment rose above the income of a person who relies only on SSI income. Recently, only nine percent of non-institutionalized people receiving SSI receive housing assistance (Consortium for Citizens with Disabilities, 2005).

Most states have not replaced the old welfare system with an alternative that enables families and individuals to obtain above-poverty employment and to sustain themselves when work is not available or possible.

HOUSING

A lack of affordable housing and the limited scale of housing assistance programs have contributed to the current housing crisis and to homelessness.

According to HUD, in recent years the shortages of affordable housing are most severe for units affordable to renters with extremely low incomes. Federal support for low-income housing has fallen 49% from 1980 to 2003 (National Low Income Housing Coalition, 2005). About 200,000 rental housing units are destroyed annually. Renting is one of the most viable options for low income people (Joint Center for Housing Studies).

Since 2000, the incomes of low-income households has declined as rents continue to rise (National Low Income Housing Coalition, 2005). In 2009, a worker would need to earn $14.97 to afford a one-bedroom apartment and $17.84 to afford a two-bedroom apartment. There has been an increase of 41% from 2000 to 2009 in fair market rent for a two-bedroom unit, according to HUD (National Low Income Housing Coalition, 2009).

The lack of affordable housing has lead to high rent burdens (rents which absorb a high proportion of income), overcrowding, and substandard housing. These phenomena, in turn, have not only forced many people to become homeless; they have put a large and growing number of people at risk of becoming homeless.

Housing assistance can make the difference between stable housing, precarious housing, or no housing at all. However, the demand for assisted housing clearly exceeds the supply: only about one-third of poor renter households receive a housing subsidy from the federal, state, or a local government (Daskal, 1998). The limited level of housing assistance means that most poor families and individuals seeking housing assistance are placed on long waiting lists. Today the average wait for Section 8 Vouchers is 35 months (U.S. Conference of Mayors, 2004).

Excessive waiting lists for public housing mean that people must remain in shelters or inadequate housing arrangements longer. In a survey of 24 cities, people remain homeless an average of seven months, and 87% of cities reported that the length of time people are homeless has increased in recent years (U.S. Conference of Mayors, 2005). Longer stays in homeless shelters result in less shelter space available for other homeless people, who must find shelter elsewhere or live on the streets. In 2007, it was found that average stay in

homeless shelters for households with children was 5.7 months, while this number is only slightly smaller for singles and unaccompanied children at 4.7 months. (The U.S. Conference for Mayors, 2007).

In 2003, the federal government spent almost twice as much in housing-related tax expenditures and direct housing assistance for households in the top income quintile than on housing subsidies for the lowest-income households (National Low Income Housing Coalition, 2005). Thus, federal housing policy has not responded to the needs of low-income households, while disproportionately benefiting the wealthiest Americans.

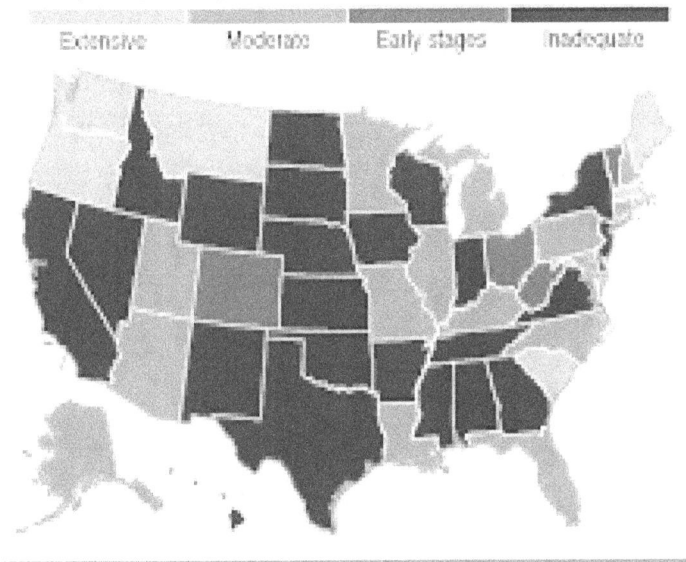

Criminalization of Homelessness

The criminalization of homelessness refers to measures that prohibit life-sustaining activities such as sleeping/camping, eating, sitting, and/or asking for money/resources in public spaces. These ordinances include criminal penalties for violations of these acts.

There are multiple types of criminalization measures which include:

Carrying out sweeps (confiscating personal property including tents, bedding, papers, clothing, medications, etc.) in city areas where homeless people live.

- Making panhandling illegal.
- Making it illegal for groups to share food with homeless persons in public spaces.
- Enforcing a "quality of life" ordinance relating to public activity and hygiene.

Unfortunately, over the past 25 years, cities across the country have penalized people who are forced to carryout out life-sustaining activities on the street and in public spaces; despite the fact these communities lack adequate affordable housing and shelter space. Ultimately, many of these measures are designed to move homeless persons out of sight, and at times out of a given city.

Why is this an issue?

Criminalization measures that punish homelessness and activities necessary to survive on the street are counterproductive to ending homelessness. Associated fines and criminal records provide greater barriers for many to becoming re-housed, and often perpetuate negative sentiments towards people who are homeless.

The US Interagency Council on Homelessness has strongly advised local governments not to enact laws criminalizing homelessness because they create additional barriers for homeless people, fail to increase access to services, and undermine the impact of service providers.

Consequently, many criminalization measures:

Violate homeless persons' constitutional rights
- *1st Amendment protection of free speech* – Laws restricting speech like begging targets speech based on content, or does not allow for alternative channels of communication.
- *4th Amendment protection from unreasonable search and seizure* – Law enforcement being allowed to destroy a homeless person's belongings.
- *8th Amendment protection from cruel and unusual punishment* – Imposing criminal penalties for engaging in necessary life sustaining activities.
- *14th Amendment protecting citizenship, due process, and equal protection* – Vague statutes which do not give a person notice of prohibited conduct and encourage arbitrary enforcement.

Exacerbate the situation
- A criminal record adds to the already difficult situation of finding employment, getting housing, or being eligible for certain services.
- Additionally, the criminalization of homelessness adds to an already overburdened criminal justice system by detaining individuals who have not committed serious crimes. One night in jail costs 3x more on average than a shelter, and law enforcement is both unprepared and incapable of handling homelessness and related issues.

Create issues of morality
There is a clear moral issue with punishing someone for carrying out life-sustaining activities in public when there are no alternatives. People who are already suffering are being punished further for suffering.

Additionally, the criminalization of homelessness is aimed at the visual ramifications of homelessness, not the root causes. Not only does it fail to address the underlying causes, but it further undermines the challenges of homelessness.

Page 13

What can be done?

Taking Action

The trend of criminalizing homelessness continues to grow. Among the 188 cities reviewed in <u>NCH's report</u>, the following increases were identified in criminalization measures:

- 7% increase in prohibitions on begging or panhandling

- 7% increase in prohibitions on camping in particular public places
- 10% increase in prohibitions on loitering in particular public places

By focusing on reversing the criminalization of homelessness, the additional obstacles homeless people face can be removed from the already difficult task of helping resolve homelessness.

Many statewide Homeless Bill of Rights have passed or are being considered that provide alternatives to criminalization and protection of the civil rights of people experiencing homelessness.

Resources

Read below for some basic facts about homelessness. For more information, check out these resources:

Further Issues that can lead to homelessness, or that face specific populations of people experiencing homelessness.

- NCH Reports and Publications on topics ranging from Criminalization to Homeless Counts.

- Archives of historical NCH Reports and resources collected by NCH relating to Homelessness and Poverty.

OTHER FACTORS

Particularly within the context of poverty and the lack of affordable housing, certain additional factors may push people into homelessness. Other major factors, which can contribute to homelessness, include the following:

Lack of Affordable Health Care: For families and individuals struggling to pay the rent, a serious illness or disability can start a downward spiral into homelessness, beginning with a lost job, depletion of savings to pay for care, and eventual eviction. One in three Americans, or 86.7 million people, is uninsured. Of those uninsured, 30.7% are under eighteen. In 2007-2008, four out of five people that were uninsured were working families. Work-based health insurance has become rarer in recent years, especially for workers in the agricultural or service sectors (Families USA, 2009).

Domestic Violence: Battered women who live in poverty are often forced to choose between abusive relationships and homelessness. In addition, 50% of the cities surveyed by the U.S. Conference of Mayors identified domestic violence as a primary cause of homelessness (U.S. Conference of Mayors, 2005).Approximately 63% of homeless women have experienced domestic violence in their adult lives (Network to End Domestic Violence).

Mental Illness: Approximately 16% of the single adult homeless population suffers from some form of severe and persistent mental illness (U.S. Conference of Mayors, 2005). Despite the disproportionate number of severely mentally ill people among the homeless population, increases in homelessness are not attributable to the release of severely mentally ill people from institutions. Most patients were released from mental hospitals in the 1950s and 1960s, yet vast increases in homelessness did not occur until the 1980s, when incomes and housing options for those living on the margins began to diminish rapidly. According to the 2003 U.S. Department of Health and Human Services Report, most homeless persons with mental illness do not need to be institutionalized, but can live in the community with the appropriate supportive housing options (U.S. Department of Health and Human Services, 2003). However, many mentally ill homeless people are unable to obtain access to supportive housing and/or other treatment services. The mental health support services most needed include case management, housing, and treatment.

Addiction Disorders: The relationship between addiction and homelessness is complex and controversial. While rates of alcohol and drug abuse are disproportionately high among the homeless population, the increase in homelessness over the past two decades cannot be explained by addiction alone. Many people who are addicted to alcohol and drugs never become homeless, but people who are poor and addicted are clearly at increased risk of homelessness. Addiction does increase the risk of displacement for the precariously housed; in the absence of appropriate treatment, it may doom one's chances of getting housing once on the streets. Homeless people often face insurmountable barriers to obtaining health care, including addictive disorder treatment services and recovery supports.

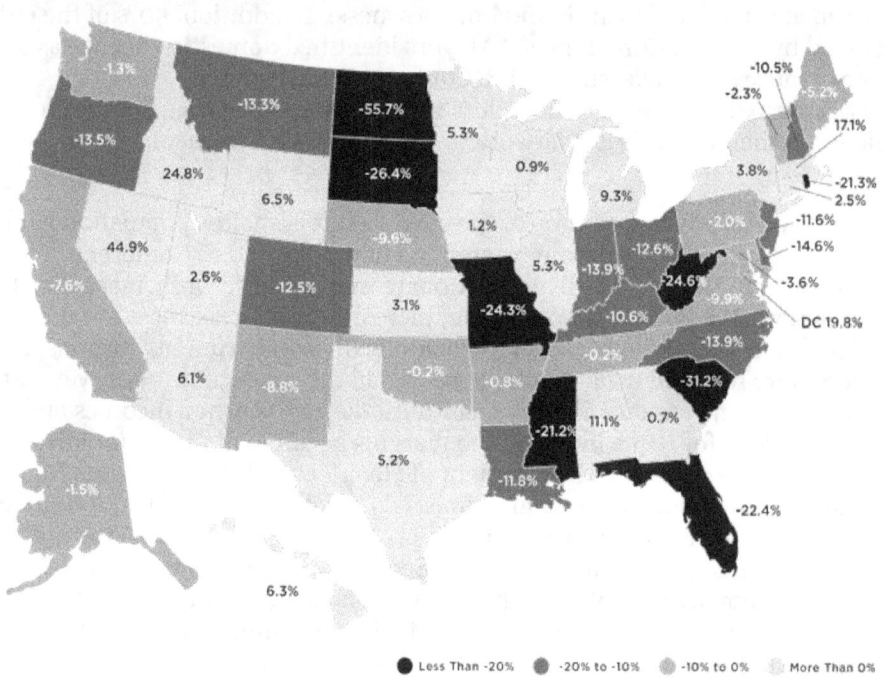

CONCLUSION

Homelessness results from a complex set of circumstances that require people to choose between food, shelter, and other basic needs. Only a concerted effort to ensure jobs that pay a living wage, adequate support for those who cannot work, affordable housing, and access to health care will bring an end to homelessness.

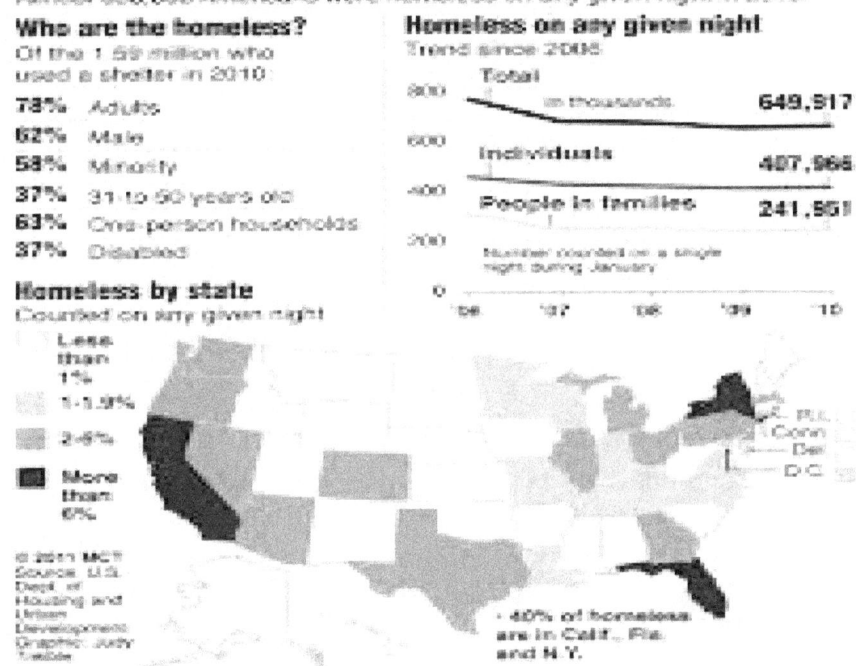

HOMELESS BILL OF RIGHTS

Years of research and advocacy around criminalization of homelessness and increasing violence committed against people experiencing homelessness has shown that added protections are needed to preserve the civil rights of people experiencing homelessness. NCH staff work to educate public officials and local advocates about the importance of passing protections for those without housing in the United States.

WHAT ARE HOMELESS BILLS OF RIGHTS?

Homeless Bill of Rights measures work to ensure that homeless individuals are:

Protected against segregation, laws targeting homeless people for their lack of housing and not their behavior, and restrictions on the use of public space.

•Granted privacy and property protections.

•Allowed the opportunity to vote and feel safe in their community without fear or harassment.

•Provided broad access to shelter, social services, legal counsel and quality education for the children of homeless families.

LOCAL HOMELESS BILL OF RIGHTS MEASURES

The following cities and states have passed or are considering homeless rights legislation:
California | Connecticut | Delaware | Illinois | Baltimore, Maryland | Minnesota | Missouri | Oregon | Puerto Rico | Rhode Island | Tennessee | Vermont | Madison, Wisconsin

Homeless Bill of Rights

Homeless Bill of Rights aims to protect life-sustaining activities

Rights to move freely, sit, sleep and have access to hygiene facilities cited in surveys of 1,300 homeless people

A coalition of over 125 social justice groups is working on a Homeless Bill of Rights to be introduced to state legislatures in an effort to end the criminalization of people who live on the streets.

Advocates working in Colorado, California and Oregon have argued that local laws have criminalized life-sustaining actions like sitting or sleeping in public places. They argue that these laws unfairly target those perceived as undesirable, including the homeless, in an attempt to push them out of public spaces.

"Imagine if every shopper in Times Square that sat down got a ticket. It would never happen. It's so blatantly racist and classist," Paul Boden, executive director of the Western Regional Advocacy Project (WRAP), told Al Jazeera, noting that those earmarked for police attention tended to be nonwhite and dressed in such a way to suggest poverty. "We're talking about laws that every single person is going to break, but only certain people have the police enforcing the laws against them."

The coalition has compiled over 1,300 interviews with the homeless and said it has identified six priority areas to be included in the Homeless Bill of Rights.

Those six are the right to move freely and sleep in public spaces without discrimination, to sleep in a parked vehicle, to eat and exchange food in public, to obtain legal counsel, to access hygiene facilities 24/7 and to use the necessity defense in any criminal prosecution.

In the coming months, the coalition will work with lawyers to develop the bill, based on the most common complaints in each of the three states and then find state representatives to sponsor the bills for legislative sessions beginning in January 2015.

icebook.com/vocalprogressives   facebook.com/lbranen

The Homeless Bill of Rights

The right to move freely and sleep in public spaces without discrimination.
The right to sleep in a parked vehicle.
The right to eat and exchange food in public spaces.
The right to hygiene facilities 24\7.
The right to legal counsel.
The right to the necessity defense in any criminal prosecution.

Demand that your elected officials pass this bill of rights into law in 2015.

Conclusion:

I, myself am homeless, I am also disabled and my servce dog helps me to cope my disability.

Me and my service dog have to sleep outdoors on the street due to none of the homeless shelters will allow my access unless if I have documentation, paperwork to prove of my service dog, which it is an ADA violation.

www.ingramcontent.com/pod-product-compliance
Lightning Source LLC
Chambersburg PA
CBHW070310190526
45169CB00004B/1571